GAME MATH

MATH 24/7

BANKING MATH

BUSINESS MATH

COMPUTER MATH

CULINARY MATH

FASHION MATH

GAME MATH

SHOPPING MATH

SPORTS MATH

TIME MATH

TRAVEL MATH

MATH 24/7

GAME MATH

JAMES FISCHER

Mason Crest

Mason Crest
450 Parkway Drive, Suite D
Broomall, PA 19008
www.masoncrest.com

Printed in the United States of America.

First printing
9 8 7 6 5 4 3 2 1

Series ISBN: 978-1-4222-2901-9
ISBN: 978-1-4222-2907-1
ebook ISBN: 978-1-4222-8918-1

Cataloging-in-Publication Data on file with the Library of Congress.

Produced by Vestal Creative Services.
www.vestalcreative.com

Contents

INTRODUCTION

How would you define math? It's not as easy as you might think. We know math has to do with numbers. We often think of it as a part, if not the basis, for the sciences, especially natural science, engineering, and medicine. When we think of math, most of us imagine equations and blackboards, formulas and textbooks.

But math is actually far bigger than that. Think about examples like Polykleitos, the fifth-century Greek sculptor, who used math to sculpt the "perfect" male nude. Or remember Leonardo da Vinci? He used geometry—what he called "golden rectangles," rectangles whose dimensions were visually pleasing—to create his famous *Mona Lisa*.

Math and art? Yes, exactly! Mathematics is essential to disciplines as diverse as medicine and the fine arts. Counting, calculation, measurement, and the study of shapes and the motions of physical objects: all these are woven into music and games, science and architecture. In fact, math developed out of everyday necessity, as a way to talk about the world around us. Math gives us a way to perceive the real world—and then allows us to manipulate the world in practical ways.

For example, as soon as two people come together to build something, they need a language to talk about the materials they'll be working with and the object that they would like to build. Imagine trying to build something—anything—without a ruler, without any way of telling someone else a measurement, or even without being able to communicate what the thing will look like when it's done!

The truth is: We use math every day, even when we don't realize that we are. We use it when we go shopping, when we play sports, when we look at the clock, when we travel, when we run a business, and even when we cook. Whether we realize it or not, we use it in countless other ordinary activities as well. Math is pretty much a 24/7 activity!

And yet lots of us think we hate math. We imagine math as the practice of dusty, old college professors writing out calculations endlessly. We have this idea in our heads that math has nothing to do with real life, and we tell ourselves that it's something we don't need to worry about outside of math class, out there in the real world.

But here's the reality: Math helps us do better in many areas of life. Adults who don't understand basic math applications run into lots of problems. The Federal Reserve, for example, found that people who went bankrupt had an average of one and a half times more debt than their income—in other words, if they were making $24,000 per year, they had an average debt of $36,000. There's a basic subtraction problem there that should have told them they were in trouble long before they had to file for bankruptcy!

As an adult, your career—whatever it is—will depend in part on your ability to calculate mathematically. Without math skills, you won't be able to become a scientist or a nurse, an engineer or a computer specialist. You won't be able to get a business degree—or work as a waitress, a construction worker, or at a checkout counter.

Every kind of sport requires math too. From scoring to strategy, you need to understand math—so whether you want to watch a football game on television or become a first-class athlete yourself, math skills will improve your experience.

And then there's the world of computers. All businesses today—from farmers to factories, from restaurants to hair salons—have at least one computer. Gigabytes, data, spreadsheets, and programming all require math comprehension. Sure, there are a lot of automated math functions you can use on your computer, but you need to be able to understand how to use them, and you need to be able to understand the results.

This kind of math is a skill we realize we need only when we are in a situation where we are required to do a quick calculation. Then we sometimes end up scratching our heads, not quite sure how to apply the math we learned in school to the real-life scenario. The books in this series will give you practice applying math to real-life situations, so that you can be ahead of the game. They'll get you started—but to learn more, you'll have to pay attention in math class and do your homework. There's no way around that.

But for the rest of your life—pretty much 24/7—you'll be glad you did!

1
DICE AND PROBABILITY

Mason loves to play games. He plays them whenever he can—at school, at home on the weekends, at friends' houses after school, on the bus. Mason will play just about every kind of game he can find.

Mason also really likes math, which is his favorite subject in school. One day in school, he learns about probability, which is the chance that something will happen. His teacher was explaining about probabilities as **expressed** in fractions.

Later, when he is playing around with some dice, he realizes that dice actually have a lot to do with probability. Mason has just discovered that most games, especially ones with dice, are based at least partly on probability. Check out the next page to see how probability relates to dice.

Mason is playing with a regular, six-sided die. Each side is labeled with one to six dots. He wants to know what the possibility of rolling a 3 is.

First he thinks about how many outcomes—or possibilities—there are when rolling a dice. The outcome is the denominator (the bottom number) of the probability fraction.

1. When he throws the die, how many outcomes are there?

To get the numerator of the fraction, you need to think about how many ways there are to get an event to happen. In this case, you want to think about how many ways Mason could roll a 3.

2. How many ways of rolling a 3 are there?

Now put those two numbers together into a probability fraction: ⅙. You could also say that Mason has a one in six chance of rolling a 3.

You can also calculate the probabilities of rolling more than one number on a die. The probability of rolling an even number, for example, is ³⁄₆. There are three ways to roll an even number, and six outcomes.

If you can reduce the fraction, you should. That way, you might be able to understand what the probability really means a little better.

3. What is ³⁄₆ reduced? Can you think of a different way of saying that probability?

Mason also has some crazy dice at home. One has ten sides, and he even has a twenty-sided die. You can do some more complicated probabilities with these dice.

The probability of rolling a 3 on a ten-sided die is ¹⁄₁₀ and on a twenty-sided die, it is ¹⁄₂₀.

4. Is ¹⁄₁₀ a bigger or smaller probability than 1/6? Why? What about a ¹⁄₂₀ probability?

5. On the twenty-sided die, what is the probability that you roll a number that is divisible by 3? You may want to list all the numbers and then count them up first.

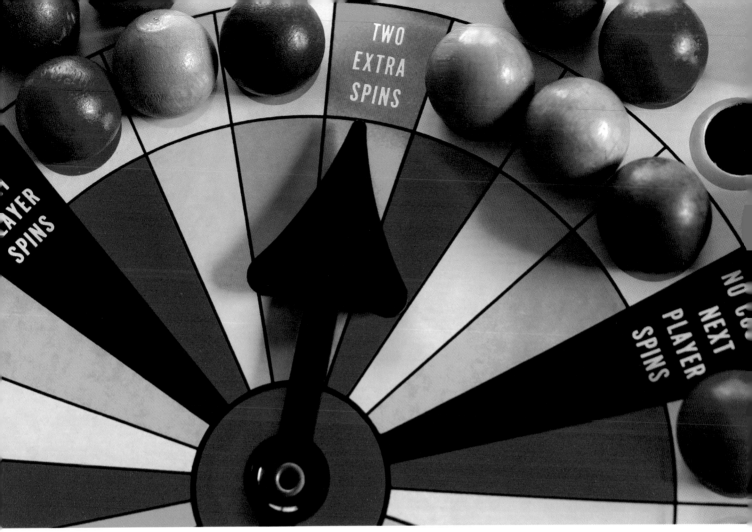

2

SPINNERS: MORE ON PROBABILITY

Many of the board games Mason plays have spinners. To move forward on the board, players spin an arrow that spins around in a circle and stops on one particular number. Just like dice, spinners rely on probability. If a spinner has six spaces, the probability of spinning a 3 is just the same as rolling a 3 on a six-sided die. The number of outcomes are the same, and the chance of getting a 3 is the same.

However, you can start to think about probability in different ways once you know the basics. Probabilities can be fractions, but they can also be decimals and percents.

You already know you can say that the probability of spinning a 3 is ⅙. The next step is to figure out how to **convert** that fraction to a decimal.

To convert a fraction to a decimal, simply divide the numerator (top number) by the denominator (bottom number).

1. What is a probability of ⅙ in decimal **numerals**? (Round your answer it to the nearest hundredth.)

Next, you can convert the decimal into a percent. Percents are parts out of 100. All you need to do is move the decimal point in a decimal over two places to the right and add a percent sign on the end.

2. What would ⅙ be as a percent?

It is up to you how you think about probabilities, but it is helpful to know all three forms.

You can even memorize some shortcuts between fractions and percents. Here are a few of the most common:

¼ = 25% = one-quarter
⅓ = 33.33% = one-third
½ = 50% = one-half
⅔ = 66.67% = two-thirds
¾ = 75% = three-quarters

Now do some more probability practice:

3. What is the probability, as a fraction, of spinning a number greater or equal to 3 on a game board with a spinner numbered 1 through 6? If it can be reduced, what does it reduce to?

4. What is that same probability as a decimal?

5. And what about the same probability as a percentage?

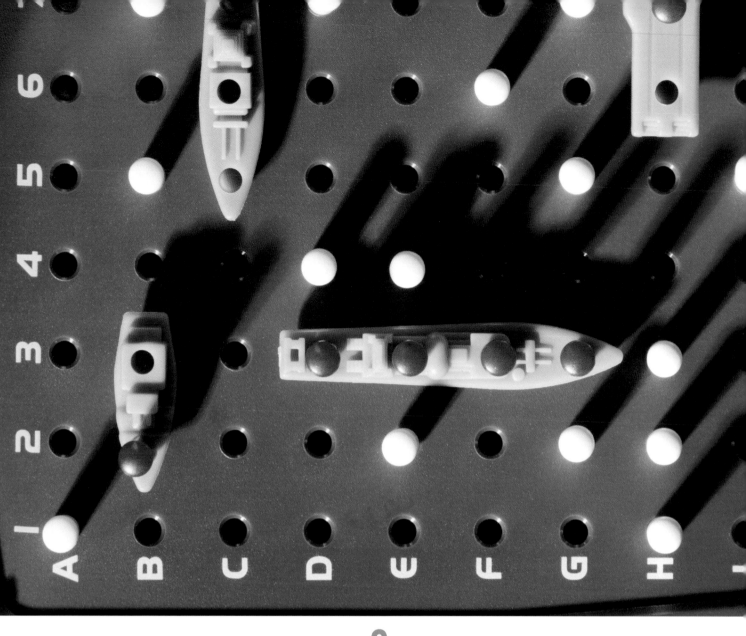

3
BATTLESHIP

Mason has the game Battleship at home, which he is teaching his younger brother Michael how to play. Mason places his own ships on the board's grid. He tells Michael to do the same thing. Then Mason explains they are going to use the grid **coordinates** to guess where the other person's ships are and sink them.

Each grid is 10 by 10. In other words, it has ten spaces across and ten spaces down. The spaces across are called rows, and the spaces down are called columns. You'll see Mason's Battleship board on the next page. His ships are marked with Xs.

	1	2	3	4	5	6	7	8	9	10
A								X	X	X
B		X		X						
C		X		X			X			
D		X		X			X			
E				X						
F										
G	X	X	X							
H						X	X	X	X	X
I										
J										

Mason lets Michael guess first. He tells him he has to identify a space on the grid by both its row and column. The rows are letters and the columns are numbers.

Michael makes a guess. He says, "G5."

1. What did Michael mean? Where should Mason put the peg to show Michael's guess? Did he get a hit?

Now Mason guesses. He guesses B7 and gets a hit! He has to take another guess and try and find the rest of the ship to sink it all.
  There are four guesses Mason could make next to get another hit.

2. What are the best guesses he could make? Why?

Mason knows he has a good chance of getting another hit, but he might miss with his guess too.
  What is the probability one of those guesses will hit a ship? You can show the probability as a fraction. First ask yourself how many choices he has. That will be the denominator. The numerator will be how many guesses he has.

3. What is the probability of getting another hit?

4
MONOPOLY

Mason and his family have game nights on Sunday nights. Everyone gets together and plays a game. Sometimes they try out new games, and sometimes they play old favorites.

Mason's dad always wants to play Monopoly. Mason hates Monopoly, though, or at least thinks he hates it. This time, his dad insists they all play. He thinks Mason really will like it if he gives it a chance. His dad also thinks it will teach him better money **management** skills, because sometimes Mason spends too much money, or loses track of where he put his cash.

They open the box and spread everything out and start playing. Soon, Mason is really getting into the game. He likes math, and he's finding that Monopoly is all about math, especially adding money. Pretty soon, he has changed his mind about the game and wants to play it every game night!

Mason is acting as the banker for this game. At the beginning, he has to give each person $1500. There are five people playing—his parents, his brother Michael, and his sister Lora.

1. How much money does he need to hand out in all?

He can't just give everyone a thousand-dollar bill and a five-hundred-dollar bill. The game doesn't even have a thousand-dollar bill.

Mason's mom gives him some bills to hand out. She gives him:

    ten $500 bills
    twenty $100 bills
    five $50 bills
    five $20 bills
    ten $10 bills
    five $5 bills
    twenty-five $5 bills.

He will need to divide the number of each of these kinds of bills by the number of players to figure out how many of each they need.

2. How many of each kind of bill should he give to each player?

Mason and his family play for a while. Eventually, he ends up spending all his money except for $55. He wants to buy St. James Place for $180.

Here is what he owns, and how much players have to pay him if they land on it:

    (orange) Tennessee Avenue, $14
    (green) Pacific Avenue, $26
    (light blue, one house) Oriental Avenue, $30
    (light blue, two houses) Vermont Avenue, $90
    (light blue, one house) Connecticut Avenue, $40

3. How much money will Mason need to buy St. James Place?

4. Are there any combinations of two spaces other players can land on which will give Mason enough money to buy St. James Place?

5
SCRABBLE

Another night, Mason and his family play Scrabble. Mason's sister, Lora, is especially good at Scrabble because she knows so many words. She loves to read all the time, and remembers just about every word she reads.

Mason is also good at Scrabble, however. He isn't as good with words as Lora is, but he pays attention to the math on the board. The board has lots of spaces marked "Double Word Score," "Triple Letter Score," and more. He knows he can use those spaces to make his words worth a lot more. He really likes to use the letters that are worth the most on the "Triple Letter Score" spaces.

The amounts the letters are worth are based on how frequently the letters are used in the English language, which is even more math! See how Mason gets his high scores on the next page.

Each of the Scrabble letters are worth 1 to 10 points. The less frequently the letters appear in English, the more they are worth. That's because they're harder to use on the Scrabble board. Here are some examples:

A is worth 1 point
W is worth 4 points
Q is worth 10 points
P is worth 3 points
G is worth 2 points
K is worth 5 points
X is worth 8 points

1. In what order would you expect the letters to be used in English, from most often used, to least often?

Now you can focus on scoring. Here's what a section of Mason's family's board looks like during the middle of the game:

Double letter score				Triple word score
		Triple letter score		
U	S	U	A Double letter score	L
Double word score				Double letter score
	Double word score			
		Triple letter score		

Mason wants to get the most points possible. He wants to use the word "quiz," because it has two 10 point letters. Q and Z are worth 10 each, U is worth 1, and I is worth 1.

The word "usual" is already on the board. He can use either "u" to build the word "quiz."

Which "u" should Mason use for more points? Fill it in on the board.

2. How many points does he get for his word?

6
CHECKERS: AREA OF A GAME BOARD

Mason likes games so much that he wants to design his own game boards. He knows it might be tricky to build a board, so he starts out with a simple game board: checkers.

A checkers board is made up of alternating red and black squares arranged into a larger square. Each red and black square is the exact same size. Mason's goal is to create a new board with green and purple squares, just for something different and to make the game more fun. He also wants to make it really big, twice the size of a normal checker board.

He'll need to figure out how to design the board. For that, he'll use length, width, and area, the size of a surface. By using these measurements he can make a professional-looking game board.

Checkerboards are squares. And squares are just rectangles where the length and width are exactly the same. A normal checkerboard is one foot (or 12 inches) long.

Mason wants to make his checkerboard twice as wide and twice as long as a normal board.

1. How long will each side be in inches?

A normal checkerboard also has 8 squares across and 8 squares down, for a total of 64 squares. The width and the length of the board are divided into 8 segments.

2. How big is each square in inches on a normal board?

3. What about on the bigger board? Are the new squares twice as big as the original ones?

Now find the area of the normal board. The equation for the area of a rectangle is:

$$area = length \times width$$

with the length being how long the rectangle is **horizontally**, and the width being how wide it is **vertically** (if you are looking at it on a piece of paper). Since a square has the same length and width, the area equation becomes:

$$area = width \times width \text{ (or length} \times \text{length)}$$

4. What is the area of a normal checkerboard in square feet? In square inches?

5. How big is the area of Mason's giant checkerboard in square feet? In square inches?

6. Is the new area twice as big as the normal area? If not, how many times bigger is it?

You have just discovered that as the sides of a rectangle double, the area quadruples!

7
ROCK, PAPER, SCISSORS

Mason and his brother and sister have to do chores every day after school. One night, they are in charge of cleaning up after dinner. One person has to wash the dishes, one person has to dry them, and one person has to put them away.

Lora washed the dishes last time, so she doesn't have to do it again. Neither Mason nor Michael wants to wash the dishes, because that seems like the most work. Mason suggests they play Rock, Paper, Scissors. The loser will have to wash the dishes. Both boys like playing games, so they make it best of seven, or whoever gets the most wins in seven games.

The next page reveals the real-life probability of Rock, Paper, Scissors, shown in charts.

According to the rules of probability, you might expect there is a ⅓ chance a player will pick rock, a ⅓ chance a player will pick paper, and a ⅓ chance a player will pick scissors. Take a look at what actually happens in Mason and Michael's game:

Mason:

Turn	Outcome
1	Rock
2	Rock
3	Scissors
4	Paper
5	Rock
6	Scissors
7	Rock

Michael:

Turn	Outcome
1	Paper
2	Rock
3	Paper
4	Rock
5	Scissors
6	Scissors
7	Paper

The probability that Mason chose Rock was ⁴⁄₇. The probability he chose Paper was ⅐. And the probability he chose Scissors was ²⁄₇.

If Michael had been a computer, he would have chosen each 1/3 of the time. But because he is a human being, he chooses Rock more often than the other two, just because he likes to. Maybe he wins more often with Rock, or he thinks it's stronger than Paper or Scissors.

1. Which of Mason's probabilities was less than ⅓? Which was more than ⅓?

2. What were the probabilities for Michael?

3. Which probabilities were less than ⅓? Which were more than ⅓?

Now figure out who had to wash the dishes. Rock beats scissors, scissors beat paper, and paper beats rock. Fill out this chart:

Turn, Who Won
1, Michael
2, Tie
3,
4,
5,
6,
7,

4. Who won? What percent of the time did he win?

8
CARD GAMES: WAR

After school, Mason goes over to his friend Diego's house. Diego particularly likes card games, so the two friends spend a lot of time playing cards.

Today, Mason and Diego play War. They start out with the simple version. They divide the cards in half and flip one over at a time. The person with the higher card gets both cards. If the two cards are the same value, they have to put three more cards face down and another card face up. Whoever has the highest card flipped up wins all the cards. The player with the most cards wins.

Then they move on to a harder version. They need to practice multiplying in their heads for school, so they make a War game out of it. Instead of one card at a time, they each flip over two cards and multiply the values together. Whoever has the highest value takes all the cards. See exactly how they play on the next page.

In lots of card games, you need to remember that face cards have number values too. Jacks are 11, queens are 12, and kings are 13. Aces are 1.

The simple version of War looks like this:

Mason	Diego
7	3
queen	10
5	9
3	4
jack	king

1. Who is winning by the end of these rounds? How many cards does each boy have from these rounds?

Then they start playing Multiplication War. They put down two cards and multiply them together to see who gets to keep the cards. This is what their game looks like. Fill in the chart:

Mason	Diego
6 x 9 =	queen x 2 =
king x ace =	9 x 4 =
3 x 5 =	ace x 5 =
7 x jack =	10 x 8 =
2 x 7 =	king x jack =

2. Who wins the first round?

3. Who is winning by the end of these five rounds?

4. How many more cards does the winner of these rounds have than the person who is behind?

9
CARD GAMES: PROBABILITY

Cards also give Mason and Diego a chance to practice probability some more. Card games are all about probability, so you might find it easier to understand probability if you play around with cards. Cards have different colors, different suits, and different numbers. Almost every card game you play will end up dealing with probability of some kind. Who knew card games could help you with math? Look on the next page to find out how.

A standard card deck has 52 cards arranged into four suits: hearts, diamonds, clubs, and spades. Hearts and diamonds are red, while clubs and spades are black.

1. What is the probability of drawing a red card? What is the reduced probability?

2. What is the probability of drawing a face card (jack, queen, king)? What is the reduced probability?

Next, look at each type of card. There are four of each number card (four 5s, four kings, etc.).

3. What is the probability of drawing one ace?

What is the probability of drawing four aces in row if you don't replace them after you draw them? You're probably thinking, "not very high," but just how tiny is that probability? This question is a little more complicated.

You'll have to calculate the probability of drawing each ace, and then multiply all those probabilities together.

You have the probability for the first ace. Now what is the probability for the second ace? You have to remember that each time you pull a card, you have one less card in the whole deck, so there is one less possible outcome. Plus, you have already drawn an ace, so you have fewer aces.

4. What are the chances you draw a second ace?

5. And what about the probability of drawing a third and fourth?

Now multiply those four probabilities together.

6. What do you get in fraction form? What about in percent form?

10
SUDOKU

One day after school, Mason sees his dad playing a word game in the newspaper. Except it's not a word game—it's a number game. Mason's dad explains he's playing Sudoku, and then he tells Mason the rules.

The puzzle is arranged in a 9-square by 9-square grid. It is further divided into nine smaller squares, which are 3 squares by 3 squares of nine even smaller squares each (see the picture on the following pages). The game has some numbers filled in randomly around the grid. The goal is to fill in the rest of the squares. You can only use the numerals 1 through 9. You can't repeat any numbers in the small box of nine squares. You also can't repeat numbers in a row or column.

Mason sees that players have to be good at adding, and they have to be good at patterns and logic. See the Sudoku puzzle and the questions that follow to get a good idea of how Sudoku works.

			8					
4				1	5		3	
	2	9		4		5	1	8
	4					1	2	
			6		2			
	3	2					9	
6	9	3		5		8	7	
	5		4	8				1
					3			

Try filling in the numbers on the third row. The third row already has a lot of numbers filled in for you.

You'll have to use a lot of trial-and-error. You can try out one number and work out a section from there. You might find it doesn't work, and have to replace that number and start the section over.

For the first square in the third row, you could try any number that isn't 1, 2, 4, 5, 8, or 9. You can also rule out 6, because 6 is already in the first column.

Next you could try the fourth square in the seventh row. The number you put there can't be 3, 5, 6, 7, 8, or 9 because they are already in that row. It also can't be 4 because 4 is in the same box of nine squares, and also in the same column.

Try to fill in the entire Sudoku puzzle. The first one you do might be hard, but don't let it frustrate you. If you keep going with them, you'll start to understand the logic behind them a little better.

11
BOWLING

Mason's friend Preeya invites him to go bowling. She knows he loves games and figures he would like to go bowling. She's right—Mason loves bowling, and he is pretty **competitive** about it.

Whenever he bowls, Mason likes to keep track of his own score. He knows the computer does it, but he likes to be sure he gets all the points he earned. He keeps track of everyone's score, not just his own.

Preeya's friend Jerome is also there. Jerome has never bowled before, so Mason explains the rules to him:

Each player gets two chances to bowl during each frame.

There are 10 frames in a game.

If you knock down all the pins, it's a strike. Strikes are worth 10 points, plus however many points you get in the next two rolls. You can't figure out your score for the frame when you get a strike until your next turn.

If you knock down all the pins using both chances, it's a spare. A spare is worth 10 points plus however many points you get on your next roll.

If you're left with at least one pin at the end of the frame, your score for the frame is however many pins you knocked down.

You get an extra roll in the last frame if you knock all the pins down.

Figure out how to score the whole game on the following page.

▶		1	2	3	4	5	6	7	8	9	10	T	

Preeya goes first. She knocks down two pins on her first roll, and gets a spare on her second. She has to wait until she rolls again in her next turn to figure out her score. On her next roll, she rolls a strike!

1. What is Preeya's score for the first frame?

On Mason's first turn, he gets a strike. He can't write his score down yet, because he has to add the value of his next two rolls. On his next two rolls, he knocks first 1 pin down, then 7.

2. What is Mason's score for his first frame?

On Jerome's first turn, he knocks down 2 and then 5 pins.

3. What is his score?

Here is the rest of what happens in the game. Use this information to fill out the score card. Use an "X" for strikes and a "/" for spares.

   Frame 1: Preeya-2, spare; Mason-strike; Jerome-2, 5
   Frame 2: Preeya- strike; Mason-1, 7; Jerome- 7, spare
   Frame 3: Preeya- 3, spare; Mason- 6, 3; Jerome- 4, 2
   Frame 4: Preeya- 4, 0; Mason- strike; Jerome- 8, 0
   Frame 5: Preeya- 7, 2; Mason- 2, spare; Jerome- 8, 1
   Frame 6: Preeya-0, 4; Mason- 4, 3; Jerome- 2, 5
   Frame 7: Preeya- 8, 1; Mason- 4, 5; Jerome- 1, 8
   Frame 8: Preeya- 0, 3; Mason-2, 0; Jerome- 4, 4
   Frame 9: Preeya- 9, spare; Mason- 0, 9; Jerome- 4, 0
   Frame 10: Preeya- 7, 1; Mason-2, 7; Jerome-9, spare, 7

4. Who won the game? How many points did he or she have?

5. How many points did the other two players have?

12
POOL

Another game Mason likes to play is pool. He just started learning it from his sister Lora. She's pretty good at pool, and she knows lots of tricks.

She and Mason are playing pool in their basement one day. She decides to tell him some of her tricks. She tells him pool is all about geometry and angles. Angles are the spaces between two lines, measured in degrees.

If you hit a pool ball with the **cue ball** at a certain angle, it will bounce away in the same angle. For example, if you hit the ball straight on, at a 180 degree angle, it would move away from you at a 180 degree angle. That would be a good shot if you could line up the cue ball, the ball, and the pocket you're trying to hit it into.

When you're playing, you won't be able to measure out the angles exactly. But you will be able to **estimate** them. The next pages show you some angles, and how to use them to become a great pool player!

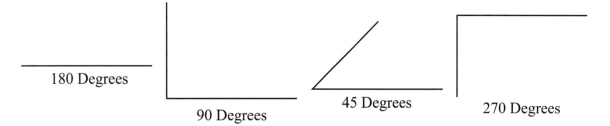

180 Degrees

90 Degrees

45 Degrees

270 Degrees

Mason starts out with an easy shot. There is a ball lined up with a pocket in the middle of the pool table's side, and the cue ball is in the same line.

Take a look at image A, where the white ball is the cue ball, and the black ball is what he is trying to put in the pocket. You can even draw the line from the cue ball, through the ball, and into the pocket to get a better sense of the angle.

1. What angle does his shot make with the ball if he lines his cue up with the cue ball, the ball, and the pocket?

You can also hit the cue ball so that it hits the ball and off the side at such an angle that it rolls into a pocket.

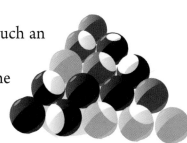

In image B, the dashed line shows the angle at which you should hit the ball on the right so it bounces off the side and into the pocket.

2. What angle is that closest to?

A third way to score is to bounce the cue ball off the side at such an angle that it bounces back and finally hits the ball, which rolls into the pocket.

The ball on the left of image B shows an example of this move.

3. What angle is it closest to?

Image A

Image B

13
VIDEO GAMES: LINEAR ALGEBRA

Mason also loves to play video games. Whenever he's not playing a board game or a word game on paper (or on the computer), he's playing a video game.

One of his favorite video games is very simple. It involves flying a spacecraft around and blasting asteroids. If you don't blast the asteroids fast enough, they end up crushing the spaceship.

This video game uses something called linear algebra. And linear algebra involves things called vectors. Vectors are simply points with a direction. As the point moves, it turns into a line in the direction it's moving.

In Mason's video game, the moving spaceship is a vector. So is the asteroid. The next pages will help you understand vectors a little more.

The big dot represents the spaceship. If it moves in the direction of the arrow, what is its vector?

The spaceship moved 3 spaces to the left. In linear algebra, that means it moved −3 spaces (negative 3). Moving to the right is positive rather than negative. The spaceship also moved 2 spaces up. In linear algebra, that means it moved 2. Moving down instead of up is negative.

The way that vectors are written is: $(-3, 2)$

Horizontal movement is written first, then vertical movement.

1. What would the vector be if the spaceship moved 1 space to the right and 4 up? Draw it in the grid.

2. How about if the spaceship moved 2 spaces to the left and 1 down? Draw it in the grid.

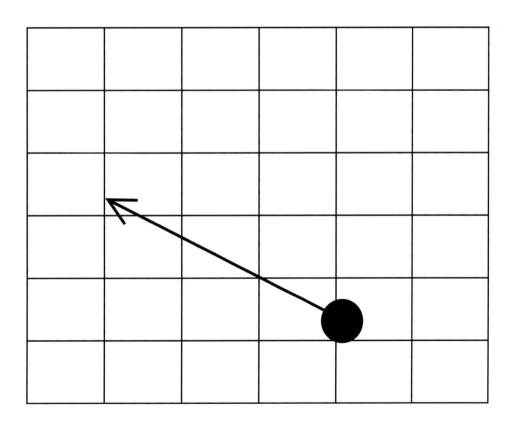

14

MORE VIDEO
GAME MATH:
SCIENTIFIC NOTATION

I n the spaceship video game, Mason tends to get high scores because he's been playing for a long time. He has to work with some pretty big numbers. Every time he reaches 1,000 points, he gets a jewel. And every time he gets 10 jewels, he gets a planet.

The goal of the game is to collect an entire solar system's worth of planets, which, in the video game world, is one hundred planets. Mason wonders how many points winning equals. He can use math to figure it out—check out the following pages.

You want to find out how many points winning the whole game equals. First, find out how many points a planet is worth.

1 planet = 10 jewels, and 1 jewel = 1,000 points.

Multiply the number of jewels you need by the number of points in a jewel. So:

1. 10 x 1,000 =

Now multiply the number of points per planet by the number of planets it takes to win the game, which is 100.

2. How many points does it take to win?

You might notice there are an awful lot of zeroes in your answers. Math gives you a handy way to write big numbers with lots of zeroes, called scientific notation. It works like this:

$10^1 = 10$
$10^2 = 100$
$10^3 = 1,000$

Now fill in the rest of the pattern:

$10^4 =$
$10^5 =$
$10^6 =$
$10^7 =$
$10^8 =$

3. How would you write the number of jewels it takes to win the video game in scientific notation?

You can also easily multiply and divide numbers written in scientific notation. Just add the exponents (the little numbers) together for multiplication, and subtract for division.

The equation to find the total number of points to win then becomes:

$10^1 \times 10^3 \times 10^2$

Add the exponents together because you are multiplying.

4. Do you get the same answer as before?

15
PUTTING IT ALL
TOGETHER

Mason never realized how connected games and math are. He likes both, so it makes
sense to him that they have a lot to do with one another.

You can see how useful math is when playing games. Math helps you understand
games better, and can even help you win! See how much you remember from all the games Mason has played.

1. What is the probability of rolling a 1 or a number greater than 4 on a six-sided die?

   Can you reduce that fraction? If so, what is its reduced form?

   What is that probability in decimal form?

   And in a percent?

2. In Monopoly, you are counting up all your money at the end of the game. Your opponent has $2,178. You have two $500 bills, six $100 bills, nine $50 bills, seven $20 bills, two $10 bills, and eleven $1 bills.

   Did you win?

   If so, by how much? If not, how much more did you need to win?

3. What is the area of a game board that is a rectangle that measures 14 inches by 22 inches?

4. You are playing multiplication War and you put down a queen and an eight. Your opponent puts down a jack and a nine.

   Who wins?

5. What is the probability that you draw a red ace out of a 52-card deck?

   What is the reduced fraction probability?

6. You are bowling and get a spare in one frame, followed by 8 pins and 1 pin in the next frame. Your friend gets a strike in one frame, followed by 2 pins and 4 pins.

   Who gets the most points for the first frame?

7. What is the vector of a video game character that runs 4 spaces left on a grid and jumps 7 spaces up?

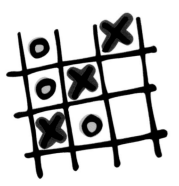

FIND OUT MORE IN BOOKS

Benjamin, Arthur and Michael Shermer. *Secrets of Mental Math*. New York: Three Rivers Press, 2006.

Clemens, Meg, Sean Clemens, and Glenn Clemens. *The Everything Kids' Math Puzzles Book*. Avon, Mass.: F + W Publishing, 2003.

Egan, Lorraine Hopping. *25 Super Cool Math Board Games*. New York: Scholastic Publishing, 1999.

Lund, Charles. *Math Games Played with Cards and Dice*. Eden Prairie, Minn.: IPMG Publishing, 2009.

FIND OUT MORE ON THE INTERNET

Get the Math: Math in Videogames
www.thirteen.org/get-the-math/teachers/math-in-videogames-lesson-plan/activities/90

How Bowling Is Scored
www.bowlingball.com/BowlVersity/how-bowling-is-scored

Johnnie's Math Page: Probability
www.jmathpage.com/JIMSProbabilitypage.html

Monopoly Math
blog.keycurriculum.com/2012/10/monopoly-math

Pool Geometry
www.coolmath-games.com/0-poolgeometry/index.html

Sudoku
www.funbrain.com/sudoku/Sudoku.html

GLOSSARY

Competitive: wanting to win.

Convert: to change into.

Coordinates: numbers used to indicate the position of a point or object.

Cue ball: the white ball used in pool to hit other balls into pockets.

Divisible: able to be divided by.

Estimate: guess.

Expressed: to represent in math with a particular form.

Frame: a turn in bowling.

Horizontally: across.

Logic: a system of using reason and math to prove.

Management: responsibility for and control of.

Numerals: symbols used to represent numbers.

Professional: serious and skilled.

Standard: normal, usual.

Trial-and-error: experimenting until an answer or solution is found.

Vertically: up and down.

Answers

1.

1. 6
2. 1
3. ½; you can also say the probability is one-half.
4. ¹⁄₁₀ is smaller, because there are more outcomes, and less of a chance any one number will be rolled. ¹⁄₂₀ is even smaller, because there are even more outcomes.
5. ⁶⁄₂₀, or ³⁄₁₀

2.

1. 0.17
2. 17%
3. ⁴⁄₆, ²⁄₃
4. 0.67
5. 66.67%

3.

1. Row G, Column 5; no, he missed the ships.
2. B6, B8, A7, C7; they are all next to his correct guess.
3. ¼

4.

1. $1,500 x 5 = $7,500
2. Two $500 bills, four $100 bills, one $50 bill, one $20 bill, two $10 bills, one $5 bill, and five $1 bills.
3. $125
4. Yes—Vermont Avenue and Connecticut Avenue.

5.

1. A, G, P, W, K, X, Q
2. 44 points.

6.

1. 24 inches
2. 1 ½ inches
3. 3 inches; yes
4. 1 square foot, 144 square inches.
5. 4 square feet, 576 square inches.
6. No, it is four times as big.

7.

1. Less: $\frac{1}{7}$, $\frac{2}{7}$; More: $\frac{4}{7}$
2. Rock = $\frac{2}{7}$, Paper = $\frac{3}{7}$, Scissors = $\frac{2}{7}$
3. Less: $\frac{2}{7}$, More: $\frac{3}{7}$

    Turn, Who Won
    1, Michael
    2, Tie
    3, Mason
    4, Mason
    5, Mason
    6, Tie
    7, Michael

4. Mason won, 43% of the time.

8.

1. Diego is winning. He has 6 cards from these rounds, and Mason has 4.
2. Mason
3. Diego
4. Diego has 4 more cards than Mason.

Mason	*Diego*
6 x 9 = 54	queen x 2 = 24
king x ace = 13	9 x 4 = 36
3 x 5 = 15	ace x 5 = 5
7x jack = 77	10 x 8 = 80
2 x 7 = 14	king x jack = 143

9.

1. $^{26}/_{52}$, ½
2. $^{12}/_{52}$, $^{3}/_{13}$
3. $^{4}/_{52}$ (or $^{1}/_{13}$)
4. $^{3}/_{51}$
5. Third: $^{2}/_{50}$, Fourth: $^{1}/_{49}$
6. $^{24}/_{6,497,400}$, 0.000369378%

10.

3	1	5	8	2	7	9	4	6
4	6	8	9	1	5	7	3	2
7	2	9	3	4	6	5	1	8
9	4	6	5	3	8	1	2	7
5	7	1	6	9	2	4	8	3
8	3	2	1	7	4	6	9	5
6	9	3	1	5	1	8	7	4
2	5	7	4	8	9	3	6	1
1	8	4	7	6	3	2	5	9

11.

1. 10 + 10 = 20
2. 10 + 8 = 18
3. 7
4. Preeya won with 108 points.
5. Mason had 105 and Jerome had 89.

12.

1. 180 degrees.
2. 45 degrees
3. 90 degrees.

13.

1. $(1, 4)$
2. $(-2, -1)$

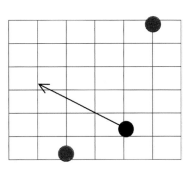

14.

1. 10,000
2. 1,000,000

$$10^4 = 10,000$$
$$10^5 = 100,000$$
$$10^6 = 1,000,000$$
$$10^7 = 10,000,000$$
$$10^8 = 100,000,000$$

3. 10^6
4. yes

15.

1. ³⁄₆; Yes, ½; .50; 50%
2. Yes; You won by $43.
3. 14 x 22 = 308 square inches
4. Your opponent wins.
5. ²⁄₅₂; ¹⁄₂₆
6. You get the most points: 18.
7. $(-4, 7)$

Index

ABOUT THE AUTHOR

James Fischer received his master's in education from the State University of New York, and went on to teach life skills to middle school students with learning disabilities. He has also written books for the Mason Crest series, Junior Library of Money.

Picture Credits

Dreamstime.com: